Hare Krishna
To mark our Silver Jubilee
We are delighted to share
Pujya Dada's secrets to
A Blissful Marriage.

Dada Shyam
With love beyond measure geetanjali & deepu
31st October 1990 - 31st October 2015

Happily Ever After

10 Secrets of a Happy Marriage

J. P. Vaswani

Published by:

GITA PUBLISHING HOUSE
Sadhu Vaswani Mission,
10, Sadhu Vaswani Path, Pune - 411 001, (India).
gph@sadhuvaswani.org

Happily Ever After

© 2015, J. P. Vaswani

ISBN: 978-93-80743-84-4

DADA VASWANI'S BOOKS
Visit us online to purchase books on self-improvement,
spiritual advancement, meditation and philosophy.
Plus audio cassettes, CDs, DVDs, monthly journals and books in Hindi.
www.dadavaswanisbooks.org

Concept: Literary Safari Inc.

Printed by: Thomson Press India Limited.

The bond of marriage unites two souls
so firmly that though they are
physically two separate entities,
their souls are merged into one harmonious whole.

- J. P. Vaswani

FOREWORD

The home is the unit of society. If the home breaks how long can society endure? Today, homes are breaking because there is a lack of the spirit of understanding. Today, brother does not understand brother. Today, children don't understand their parents. Today, husbands do not understand their wives.

Listen to the conversations of the world. Listen to the conversations of the nations. Listen to the conversations of individuals, and you will find that the spirit of understanding is lacking. Listen to the conversation of the couples. I have heard them and do you know what I call them? I call them "dialogues of the deaf". Each one is out to set forth his ideas to defend himself, to justify his position, to make himself look greater than he truly is, and to accuse the other person.

Just think of the little things, the petty things, over which we quarrel in our homes.

A husband was taking his breakfast when his wife emerged out of the bathroom. She looked annoyed. Her husband asked her, "Has something happened, you look so annoyed?"

"No, no don't ask me," she replied. "Let things be as they are."

"No," said the husband. "You were so cheerful, you were cracking jokes before you went to the bathroom, now you have come out of the bathroom you look so annoyed. What is the reason?"

Finally the wife said, "Alright, if you ask me, then let me tell you. How many times have I not told you never to press the toothpaste tube at the middle? But you never listen to me! You always do it."

And so a quarrel ensued.

The husband said, "So what if I press the toothpaste tube at the middle. After all, toothpaste tubes are bought out of the money that I earn with the sweat of my brow."

And the quarrel went on and on.

This problem had a very simple solution. The wife could have easily got a separate toothpaste tube for herself and let the husband keep on pressing his toothpaste as often as he likes.

But there is the ego problem. The ego is something which will never, never, never give in. And therefore we have quarrels in our families today. The spirit of understanding is lacking.

Here is another true story. There is a couple. The wife cannot sleep at night until first she has read something. Otherwise she keeps on turning and tossing in bed. However, the husband cannot sleep if there is a light on in the room. So when they both retire, the wife switches on the light. Immediately the husband gets up and says, "Dare you!" He switches off the light. And, so, a quarrel ensues.

This quarrel goes on and on until both of them, feeling exhausted, go off to sleep with negative thoughts and an intent to restart the quarrel the next morning at the earliest opportunity.

Every problem has a solution. This problem too could easily be solved. The wife could easily have got for herself a bedside spotlight which would not disturb the husband in his sleep. But, again, there is the problem of the ego.

This is the condition in so many of our homes today.

A couple from New York met me. The wife complained, "My husband is a workaholic. He keeps on working and working, and he pays no attention to me. I feel ignored. I feel neglected and our marriage is about to crack."

I met the husband. He was a very fine man. He did not defend his position. He said, "What my wife says is only too true, but from now on I promise to take her out once every week, one evening every week." He said, "Every Wednesday evening I will take her out. I will take her to the movies, I will take her to the club, I will take her wherever she likes." And he does take her out. Every Wednesday evening he takes her out.

That is a step in the right direction. But the husband makes no attempt to understand his wife. It is this spirit of understanding that is needed. We may go out every evening together, we may live under the same roof, for years together, but if there is no spirit of understanding we don't draw close to each other. It is this closeness that is needed.

This feeling of closeness converts a house into a home. It is this closeness that is lacking in our families today. Think of our outstanding intelligent cultured families, think of our leaders of society, big businessmen, successful industrialists, learned professors, they make no attempt to understand their spouses. It is this spirit of understanding that leads to closeness and once you have lived closely with each other, all the changing vicissitudes of life will not make you drift apart.

There are 10 simple gifts of understanding that you can offer to your life partner. Practice them together and watch as they transform your house into a happy home!

~ J. P. Vaswani

Make a Daily Affirmation

Throughout this book you will find short and simple affirmations that can strengthen your relationships.

Scientific research shows that a key to changing the way you think is through frequent and vigorous mental exercise: the daily affirmation. An affirmation is a short, uplifting thought that you repeat to yourself on a regular basis.

What are the convictions you have about your marriage or about yourself? By repeating these uplifting thoughts, you can train your brain to think and behave more positively. At first, it doesn't matter if you don't believe what you are saying! The whole purpose of using daily affirmations is to change the way you think, so keep repeating them, even if your initial doubts creep up.

There are also blank lines to create your own affirmations.

STEP 1: WRITE YOUR AFFIRMATION

There are blank lines throughout the book for you to write your own affirmations. The wording should be customized for your life circumstances and the way you would like to think. A good way to start is by identifying your problem or typical negative situation. For example, if you find yourself thinking, "He never listens to me," an appropriate affirmation would be, "He will listen to me."

STEP 2: SAY YOUR AFFIRMATION

Don't rush through it. Breathe and say it to yourself— mentally or aloud— slow and steady. Your affirmation will be more effective if you say it slowly, pausing in between each repetition to let it sink in. Inhale the positivity. Exhale your old way of thinking. Imagine that you are trying to convince someone else that it is true. Don't mumble it too fast just to get it out of the way. Choose a time that becomes part of your daily routine–when you first wake up, before meals, or right before bed.

STEP 3: ENJOY THE FRUITS OF YOUR LABOUR

Don't expect your affirmations to change your negative thinking or a difficult situation overnight. Changing the way you approach a situation is hard, slow work. It could take weeks or months to feel yourself turn over to a new perspective. Have faith that over a period of time your diligent recitations will pay off and come to mind spontaneously as you go through your daily life. You'll also be more aware of the negative thinking that used to be so automatic.

CONTENTS

The First Secret...

Avoid the next quarrel

You have already quarreled so many times!

So, I cannot say avoid the FIRST quarrel.

I can only say: Come what may, avoid the NEXT quarrel.

IN REAL LIFE ...

I once met a couple that has a reputation of being short tempered. They both had the tendency to be angry at the least excuse. Nevertheless, when they celebrated their golden anniversary, they declared, "During all these 50 years, we have never quarreled with each other. Not even once!"

The people were amazed. Of course, they wanted to know their secret.

They said, "The secret is a simple one. When we married, we made a pact with each other that both of us would never lose our temper at the same time. We resolved that if one of us got angry, the other one would be patient. We have held on to that agreement through these 50 years and that is why our marriage has been such a happy one."

THE TAKEAWAY

Come what may, both partners should not be, at the same time, in a mood to quarrel. If one of you is in a mood to quarrel, the other one should be patient. Your turn will come at the right time.

Try this at Home

Don't give up on yourself if you cannot avoid the next quarrel. Here are 3 simple things that you can do to get back on track.

1. Don't fall asleep on the quarrel

Even, perchance, if you do quarrel, see that you don't let the sun set on your quarrel.

2. Don't wake up to a quarrel

If it so happens that you get up in the middle of the night and quarrel, then don't let the sun rise on your quarrel. Make up before sunrise or sunset.

3. DON'T BE TOO PROUD TO SAY "I'M SORRY"

Giving in does not mean giving up. You do not become small if you realise your mistake and go and apologise to your spouse. One has to realise that nobody is perfect. We all have our share of unpleasant quirks, foibles, and eccentricities. An important part of marriage is to understand and make allowances for the failings of your partner. Every marriage will have its share of misunderstandings and differences. But the wise learn from them.

Try this daily affirmation: "I will be patient with my partner."

ASK DADA

Is there such a thing as a healthy quarrel?

Yes, there is. A healthy quarrel is when you can have a brief, honest exchange of angry feelings, followed by a brief 'cooling off' period and then, all is forgiven and forgotten!

If I stay quiet and wait for my turn during a fight, I feel like I am giving in.

Giving in does not imply giving up. Unfortunately, when a quarrel arises, couples just speak in anger – and respond with more anger. If you wish the 'black mood' to end quickly, both of you must learn to control yourself. When you exercise self-control, you are cutting off fuel to the fire, which is sure to die quickly.

A marriage without any fights would be boring. And besides, which marriage is perfect?

A marriage in which the partners claim that they have never been angry would be a very dull and boring marriage indeed. And, constant quarreling can damage any relationship. But if the disagreement is constructive and handled in the right way, it can actually strengthen the marriage.

MEDITATION MOMENTS

When you are in the right, you do not need to lose your temper. When you are in the wrong, you cannot afford to lose it.

~ Mahatma Gandhi

POWER UP YOUR DAY WITH YOUR OWN DAILY AFFIRMATION.

I let go of _____

_____

_____

The Second Secret...

BE A GOOD LISTENER

Never interrupt your spouse when he or she is talking.

Let them prove their point.

Let them finish!

LIFE IMITATES ART

In Voltaire's story *Candide*, the hero and heroine dream and plan their future lives together. Unfortunately, both of them are too self-centered to listen to the other's ideas.

Her dreams are all about material wealth—rubies, pearls, marble palaces with extensive gardens and swimming pools. His dreams are idyllic—to live simply on a few acres of land, with a pig, a cow and a kitchen garden to putter about in.

Naturally, disaster and disillusion ensue for the couple.

THE TAKEAWAY

Misunderstandings due to poor listening have caused a lot of misery in many marriages. When you fail to listen to your spouse, you can cause pain and unhappiness. This leads to loneliness, alienation, hurt, and wasted moments of precious life.

But, there is hope! Listening is an art that we can all learn!

Practice Makes Perfect: The Art of Listening

It has been said that listening is your window into your spouse's world. It is an opportunity for you to make your spouse realise that his or her concerns are important to you. Here are some simple ways to become a better listener.

1. Make Eye-contact

Listening involves both hearing and paying attention. Let your partner be aware that you are listening. Do not yawn, look at your watch, or fidget in your seat. Do not watch TV, message a friend, read a book, or look at photos on Facebook. Look at your partner when he or she is talking.

2. Offer verbal feedback

Acknowledge what your partner is telling you. A phrase like "I know what you mean, honey" can make a world of difference. So can phrases like "Go on, I am listening" or "I understand what you are saying" or "Tell me more". These simple words demonstrate your emotional receptivity to your partner.

3. DON'T INTERRUPT

How many times have you heard your partner say, "But, let me finish!" He or she is trying to make a point, but is interrupted so often. Why not listen to your partner's full story first—before you react? Exercise restraint so that he or she can finish speaking. Even if your impulse is to defend yourself. Even if you have the perfect counter point.

4. "WHAT I AM HEARING IS..."

After your partner finishes speaking, you can summarize or restate what you have heard. Starting with the simple phrase, "What I am hearing is..." sends the message that you have listened carefully. You also open the doorway to clear up any misunderstanding by asking, "Is that what you meant?" Your partner will appreciate your effort to seek clarifications.

Try this daily affirmation: "Everyday and in every way I am getting better and better at listening to my partner."

Ask Dada

She's always talking and I do nothing but listen. How is that fair?

You may be hearing and listening, but are you listening effectively? Effective listening involves much more than hearing and listening. You observe carefully, interpret your partner's mood, action and body language, clarify and confirm the message you receive and then respond with sympathy and understanding. Effective listening is of critical importance in a marriage.

What about speaking? Are there any rules for healthy speech in a relationship?

Yes! As a very wholesome principle of life, learn to ask yourself: "Are the words I am going to utter now, better than silence?"As it is said, speech is silver, silence is golden. Speak only that which is good, pleasant, true and not hurtful to others.

MEDITATION MOMENTS

O Lord, I keep on talking and talking as though I have mouths all over the body. When shall I cease from doing so? When shall I enter the silence within?

~ Avvayar

POWER UP YOUR DAY WITH YOUR OWN DAILY AFFIRMATION.

I can _____

_____

_____

The Third Secret...

APPRECIATE YOUR SPOUSE

Take time to talk to one another. Share your feelings. Express your appreciation for one another. Give a compliment!

These are the small things that nourish and strengthen the bonds of marriage over time.

IN REAL LIFE ...

There was a young lady who loved to cook. After a long day of work, she came home one day and worked very hard to present a special delicacy to tickle her husband's palate. After taking his first bite, her husband murmured, "For a change, the food is good today."

THE TAKEAWAY

Consider how the whole scenario would change if the husband, upon taking his first bite, says to his wife, "That's a new recipe, isn't it? I liked it." Compliments assure us that we are loved and appreciated. When you express your appreciation of your spouse, you give recognition of her strengths, or prop him up where he needs most support. An honest compliment is simple and uttered from the heart. It costs nothing to give, but its worth is inestimable!

The Magic of Appreciation

When we appreciate others, we help draw out the best that is in them. Here are some simple practices to try.

1. Utter the Magic formula

"Honey, where would I be without you?" These seven words can create a new atmosphere in your home. They must be spoken at least once every day. I have shared this formula with hundreds of people around the world and they come back to me—again and again—and tell me about the new world that they have created in their home. Say them with deep emotion and feeling of the heart. Not like a robot!

2. Write little notes of appreciation

It could be for a special meal, a kind word he has said, or just patient listening that she gave you. The note can say, "I'm so glad to have you." Or, "I'm so proud of you," or even, "I like to hear you sing in the shower." Think of the big difference a small note like this would make in your day!

3. ASK, "HOW WAS YOUR DAY?"

Nowadays both partners work outside the home. Both are pursuing careers and living hectic, professional lives. It is even more important to take time out to talk to each other, share feelings, and express appreciation. This simple question can open the doorway for a real conversation and show that you really care.

4. COUNT YOUR BLESSINGS

Make time as a couple, to list and talk about the things in life for which you are grateful. This practice will get you through difficult times. It will help you remember the blessings conferred upon you through marriage.

Try this daily affirmation: " I nourish myself by appreciating my partner."

ASK DADA

My wife says that I should know by now that she loves me, so why does she need to say it. But, I still like to hear nice things said about me. Am I being childish?

It is a natural human need. All of us yearn to be appreciated. Compliments assure us that we are loved and appreciated. Mark Twain once said that he could go on for about two months without a good compliment—but no longer. A compliment not only makes you happy, but it also builds up your self-esteem.

My husband likes to fix things that go wrong in the house, but he is not very handy. Things always get worse. He says that I am very harsh with him, but I am just being honest. I don't want to resort to flattery or be insincere and tell him that he's doing a good job.

Each of us has so many positive qualities. When you take the trouble to identify these 'positives' in your spouse and compliment him on them, you will not only make him happy but you will also build up his self-esteem. Sometimes it's not what you say, but how you say it. And, what you say along with it. For example, you can say, "I really appreciate the time you took to try to fix this. It shows me how much you care. But what do you think about having someone else do it next time?" Or, you can compliment him on the small things he does do well around the house.

MEDITATION MOMENTS

If you haven't all the things you want, be grateful for the things you don't have that you wouldn't want.

~ Unknown

POWER UP YOUR DAY WITH YOUR OWN DAILY AFFIRMATION.

I value my partner for _____

_____

_____

_____.

The Fourth Secret...

KEEP YOUR LOVE FRESH!

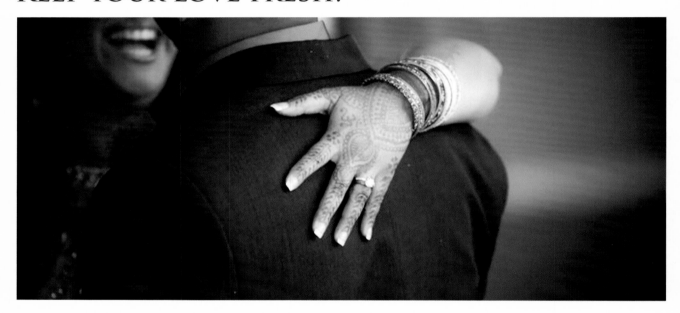

The most happy marriage may become dull and colourless if you begin to take each other for granted.

Listen to the emotional needs of your partners. Absorb the spirit of their conversation. Appreciate their dreams and aspirations. Learn to support and encourage them in every way.

IN REAL LIFE ...

I met a couple who were leading "full, active lives", as they put it. The husband is a busy executive who jet-sets all over the world. He attends seminars, conferences, and business meetings. He entertains clients and consultants at fancy restaurants. On weekends, he relaxes by playing golf with friends.

As for the wife, she is into yoga and fitness. She visits fashion designers. She is a regular member of the Ladies' club where she plays cards with her friends everyday. She is also passionate about designing jewelry and hopes to open her own outlet soon.

This couple is beginning to go in separate revolving circles. They are in danger of becoming married strangers. They live under the same roof, eat at the same table, and share a bed every night... but they are drifting apart.

THE TAKEAWAY

Emotional and physical independence comes easily to men and women these days. I think there is something valuable about a relationship where husband and wife need each other, and are vulnerable without the other's support.

This couple must spare more time to be in each other's company. They should spend more time with the children. They should loosen their schedules and deadlines so that their marriage does not suffer. They should work for change.

Yes, it takes work to keep love fresh!

It takes effort.

HOW CAN YOU KEEP YOUR LOVE FRESH?

It was a wise woman who remarked, "Of course, my husband and I take each other's love for granted. We are safe and secure in our love. But we never take each other for granted!" Here are some tips for keeping the flame of love alive in your marriage.

1. SUPPORT YOUR PARTNER IN PURSUING HIS OR HER INTERESTS

If your wife enjoys playing the piano, encourage her to pursue her interest. Take her to concerts. Find her a music teacher. Ask her to play a song for you. Whatever special talent or interest your spouse has, encourage it, appreciate it.

2. GET TO KNOW YOUR SPOUSE A LITTLE BETTER EACH DAY

Consider your spouse rare and fascinating. Try to get to know him a little bit more each day. Take time to study her. Ask questions such as, "Tell me something I don't know about you." Or, find out about his or her childhood. It's easy to assume that you know everything there is to know about our life partners. But we are human beings. We are always changing. What new thing will you learn about your partner today?

Try this daily affirmation: "It is easy for me to express love and in return, it is easily expressed back to me."

ASK DADA

When my husband comes home from work, I'm so tired after a long day with the children. He gets upset if I'm watching TV or in bed, even though I have dinner ready and on the table. Why can't he understand that I also need to rest?

There was a woman. One day, a husband returned home from work, weary and stressed. As he entered the home, his wife took his briefcase and said lovingly, "Would you like a cold drink first or will you have dinner right away? You look exhausted." The husband was overcome with this gesture of love and caring. It was the complete attention that touched him. What if you turned off the TV or hung up the phone and said hello? Give him a hug or a kiss? In a relationship, the other is always looking for reassurance that they are important to you.

When I come home from work, I just want to eat my dinner in silence and watch TV. I am too tired to talk. I've explained this to my wife over and over again, but she always gets angry and spoils my evening with her complaints. She says she feels just like a piece of furniture. How can I help her to understand?

Consider how the whole scenario would change if you, upon entering, just asked your wife, "How was your day, honey? Tell me about it." If you're too tired to talk, you can just listen.

MEDITATION MOMENTS

Perhaps love is the process of my leading you gently back to yourself.

~ **Antoine de Saint-Exupéry**

POWER UP YOUR DAY WITH YOUR OWN DAILY AFFIRMATION.

*I breathe love into*_____

_____.

The Fifth Secret...

DO NOT EXPECT PERFECTION FROM EACH OTHER!

No man or woman is ever perfect.

Marriage involves the coming together of two imperfect human beings.

Therefore, accept your spouse for what he or she is, not for what he or she would be, could be, or should be.

IN REAL LIFE ...

Young people today expect too much from married life. They look for material comfort, complete fulfillment, and a sense of achievement.

Young girls dream of the perfect man—handsome, kind, highly qualified, wealthy, and intelligent. As for young men—they dream of tall, slim, fair princesses who look like film stars but can cook like their grandmothers.

At first, life does seem like a fairy tale. But over time, the reality of life cannot match up to one's fantasies. It is then that couples suffer from disappointment and frustration. They feel cheated. They think they have made a ghastly mistake.

THE TAKEAWAY

They have made a mistake. That mistake was to expect too much from marriage in the first place. It is good for young men and women to go into marriage with a clear eyed realisation that life has its limitations, and marriages have their store of problems.

As human beings, none of us is perfect. Frailties and imperfections abound in each of us. We succumb to anger, falsehood, prejudice, and hate so easily and so often.

When we learn to love each other in spite of these failings, we truly rise in love, instead of falling out of love.

PERFECTION BEGINS WITH YOU

I know some people who pride themselves on being 'perfectionists'. This is a wonderful thing so long as they aim for perfection in all that they say and do. But when they begin to demand perfection (as per their standards) from their partners, they are only asking for trouble. Train your eagle eyes on yourself and try to become the perfect partner yourself. Here are a few simple ways to start.

1. DON'T LOOK FOR LOVE. ALWAYS LOOK WITH LOVE

Love cannot flourish under a critical gaze. Look at your partner with tolerance and understanding, forgiveness and optimism. It's not always easy, but try to find the vein of gold hidden within your partner. Then, figure out a way to do everything you can to expose that gold.

2. CHOOSE YOUR BATTLES

Try not to interfere in your partner's every choice and action. I've met spouses who say, "This is what you should wear. This is how you should talk. You should not do this. You must not go there." Such demands are excessive. They only lead to nasty wars. Instead of constantly nagging your spouse, make a list of your expectations of your partner, and study them. Which ones are really important to the quality of your marriage? Focus on those. Talk about them together. Then, ask your partner to do the same for you.

3. HIGHLIGHT THE POSITIVE

Instead of always saying, "I hate it when ...," how about saying, "I love it when ..." And, don't forget to speak gently. Even a word, a gesture, a wrong tone of voice can cause friction in a marriage.

Try this daily affirmation: "I accept my spouse for what he or she is, not for what he or she would be, could be, or should be."

ASK DADA

I've heard you say that we should practice selfless love. What is the difference between selfish and selfless love?

Selfless love seeks to understand, accept, sympathize, forgive, and appreciate. Selfish love, on the other hand, makes demands and nourishes impossible expectations. Do you want a blessed union? Practice selfless love! The truth is, happy marriages are based on the principle of give and take. One of the fundamental requirements of a successful marriage is to accept your partner with love and understanding—to learn to live and love selflessly.

How can I be a best friend to my spouse?

Henry Ford gave a good answer to this question. "A best friend is the person who brings out of you the best that is in you," he said. When you encourage and support your partner, you will evolve and mature and learn to be a true friend. And marriage, after all, is about friendship despite all the troubles, the odds, the bitter and sweet experiences of life. These will help you emerge steadier and stronger in love.

MEDITATION MOMENTS

Call me not perfect. Alone the father in heaven is perfect.

~ Jesus Christ

POWER UP YOUR DAY WITH YOUR OWN DAILY AFFIRMATION.

I practice selfless love by _____

_____

_____.

The Sixth Secret...

Be a good forgiver

To make marriage a success, to make it a source of happiness and harmony, you have to forgive much.

It is the prerogative of marriage to give and give and give — and forgive — and never be tired of giving and forgiving.

IN REAL LIFE ...

There was a man who had a dear friend. They were almost like brothers. One day, this friend betrayed him. It was too much to bear so he vowed never to speak to him again.

Many years later, on his death bed, he remembered this friend of his. Knowing that he was about to die, he sent for him. "Let's make amends before I leave this body," he said. "Now that I am about to pass away, I forgive everything and I forget everything. I forgive you."

The two men hugged one another.

Then, just as his friend was about to leave, the dying man called out, "Mind you, this stands good only if I die. If I continue to live, I will not forgive. I will not forget."

THE TAKEAWAY

Don't forgive like that man!!! That is not forgiveness. "I can forgive, but I cannot forget," is only another way of saying, "I will not forgive." Your forgiveness must be total.

Just as no human being is perfect, no marriage is perfect either. Misunderstandings, accidents, and quarrels will inevitably occur. These may be over in a flash, but then, bitter memories linger.

Forgiveness in marriage is not logical or methodical. It is simple and straightforward. You accept your spouse's shortcomings and you continue to love.

4 STEPS ON THE PATH OF FORGIVENESS

1. ACCEPT AN HONEST APOLOGY

You've been hurt. You're angry. It's tempting to hold on, but where will that get you? Why not take a deep breath and accept the apology that is being offered to you. It is honest. It is sincere. It is in good faith. Accept it! When you forgive your spouse, you both feel better! Bitterness and anger are wiped out. Thus forgiveness is its own reward.

57

2. DON'T WAIT UNTIL IT'S TOO LATE

Many times, we recognize the worth of people only when they are gone. Let us appreciate our dear ones while they are still with us. Forgive while you can.

3. DON'T HARBOUR AN UNFORGIVING, UNFORGETTING ATTITUDE IN YOUR HEART

"You forgot my birthday last year. You did not let me take that golfing weekend with my friends. You made me do that." What will be gained by holding on to such feelings? Let go!

4. FORGIVE YOURSELF

Forgiveness needs to be extended not only to your spouse. It requires a healing process inside you so that you do not feel any bitterness or resentment about what happened.

Try this daily affirmation: "I easily forgive others and am easily forgiven."

ASK DADA

How many times shall I forgive my wife? Shall I forgive her 7 times?

No! You must forgive 70 times 7! 70 times 7 is 490 times, which means that you must forgive without counting.

I have been forgiving my husband and received nothing in return. I can forgive no longer!

Continue to forgive without expecting anything in return. Forgiveness is the characteristic of selfless, unconditional love. It has rightly been described as the 'emotional disarmament' in marriage.

MEDITATION MOMENTS

Forgiveness is a funny thing. It warms the heart and cools the sting.

~ William Arthur Ward

POWER UP YOUR DAY WITH YOUR OWN DAILY AFFIRMATION.

I forgive and release _____

_____.

The Seventh Secret...

UNDERSTAND ONE ANOTHER

Understanding is a complex art. It requires kindness and empathy. It involves tolerance and loving patience. It includes a healthy respect for each other's interests.

As you make the effort to understand your spouse, you grow in the understanding of yourself. You acquire wisdom and patience. And, you learn to avoid those needless misunderstandings that waste so much time and energy.

The great secret of human happiness lies in understanding.

Kamla and Kishore are a working couple. Kamla works in a bank and Kishore is a teacher. One day, Kamla was held up in the office due to the yearly closing of accounts. She asked her husband to buy some milk, bread, and vegetables on his way home. "I'll make toasted sandwiches and tea for dinner," she said to him on the phone.

When Kamla got home at 8 pm, she was irked to see Kishore was relaxing in front of the television. The shopping bag on the kitchen counter was empty. "Good to see you home so early," he greeted her cheerfully.

Kamla was tired, hungry and angry. She shut herself up in the bedroom. How selfish and careless Kishore was. She would teach him a lesson. Since there was nothing to make dinner with, he would just have to fast!

After a half hour, Kamla emerged from her bedroom to get herself a drink of water. Lo and behold, there in the fridge was a new packet of milk! "Oh good, I'll just make myself some tea after all," she thought. And when she turned on the stove, there she saw a plate full of sandwiches. Kishore had already lavishly sliced tomatoes, onions, and cheese between the slices of bread. Oh, how kind and sweet and loving her husband was! Kamla's eyes filled with tears of remorse.

THE TAKEAWAY

This is how misunderstanding affects attitudes. When you misunderstand your spouse, you look at a situation with jaundiced eyes. Then when the truth dawns on you, you see things completely differently.

4 Ways to Grow in Understanding

1. Be humble

Did you know that the word understand is actually related to its literal meaning, that is to stand under something? When you stand under something, you are able to observe it from the bottom to the top. You look at it from a fuller perspective. Therefore to understand your partner, you have to be willing to stand under him or her! You have to be willing to be humble. This is not a sign of weakness. Standing under does not mean that your partner can possess and control you. Absolute control over another person is inhuman and undesirable. As the wise saying goes, "The bird of paradise alights only upon the hand that does not grasp." Standing under is a sign of strength.

2. Accept each other as equal

It is vital in a happy marriage for both partners to accept each other as equals. Marriage is a wonderful bond of companionship where no partner has to feel inferior or superior. If you do not treat your partner as an equal—beware, there is something wrong with your attitude! Love, understanding, and mutual respect are the fundamentals of a happy marriage—and that exists only among equals.

3. Do as you would be done by

When you make this command a part of your daily life, you grow in empathy. Empathy is nothing but understanding the other's point of view. Do you feel that you should never be hurt or upset or let down by your partner? Extend the same courtesy to him or her. For empathy is based on mutual respect. We will develop the spirit of empathy when we learn to step out of our rigid, inflexible positions and view the world from another's perspective.

4. Be tolerant

True love enhances. It does not degrade or devalue. In this age of individuality and self-assertion, tolerance is nothing but the sincere effort to understand, appreciate, and respect your partner's beliefs and habits. If you truly love someone, how can you belittle that person? Insults and caustic comments will never change anyone for the better. They will only aggravate the situation.

Try this daily affirmation: "I foster in myself the power to understand my partner's need rather than judge him by his deed."

ASK DADA

My husband really doesn't have a good sense of style, but he takes offence when I give him suggestions on how to dress.

Many people suffer from a needless compulsion to change their partners. What a sad thing it is when we can only find fault with people whom we love. People have one thing in common. They are all different. You may nag, cajole, beg, and shape your husband into the exact man you want him to be. But then you will have a new problem like the woman I met. "He's just not the man I married," she sighed in frustration!

I have a personal gym in the basement and devote time to my fitness every morning and on weekends. My wife complains and says I don't have time for her.

A happy and healthy relationship requires that you should give each other the opportunity to pursue those interests which your spouse does not share. What are the activities that matter to your wife? Help her to create the space and find the time for these activities within your home and marriage. If she can find the space to maintain her own individuality and creativity, maybe she will not feel this way.

MEDITATION MOMENTS

With all thy getting, get understanding.

~ The Book of Proverbs

POWER UP YOUR DAY WITH YOUR OWN DAILY AFFIRMATION.

I can try to understand why _____

_____

_____.

The Eighth Secret...

DEVELOP A HEALTHY SENSE OF HUMOUR

A little laughter can change the day. A child's happy giggle, a joke shared between a couple, or even a chuckle over a funny event in the past! When things get you down, do not explode in anger and stress. Find a reason to laugh – and you will see that anger and stress simply melt away. Truly, a good laugh can let sunshine and warmth into your home and your marriage!

IN REAL LIFE ...

There was a husband. He was tall and hefty. His wife was short and slim. One day they got into an argument. The husband lost his temper and said to his wife: "If I liked, I could swallow you up." The wife had a sense of humour. She laughed as she said: "If you swallowed me up, you would have more brains in your belly than in your head!"

THE TAKEAWAY

If two people have to live with each other, they must learn to laugh and make each other laugh.

Unfortunately married couples today seem to be losing the ability to laugh with each other, or indeed laugh at themselves. The world seems to have grown very serious nowadays. We tend to look at life solemnly. We have even begun to equate maturity with seriousness.

Where did all the fun and banter go?

Each one of us has some oddities, some unpleasant quirks or weaknesses. We can always find a way to laugh about these.

That is why I often tell my married friends: It is a sad day, an incomplete day in your life, if you have not laughed together heartily at least 3 times!

TURN A FROWN UPSIDE DOWN

Humour is an all-round tonic. It promotes your physical, mental, and emotional well-being. Here are 3 simple ways to bring a sense of humour into your home and marriage.

1. SET YOUR INNER CHILD FREE

There is a little child in all of us who never ever grows old—no matter what our age. He needs to be coaxed to come out and play. True, life is a serious business and requires our deliberate consideration and thoughtful response. But a little fun and laughter now and then does plenty of good for everyone!

2. PLAY GAMES

Experts tell us that play is therapeutic. It brings out our spontaneity and erases our self-consciousness. Don't get trapped in daily chores, rituals, work, and TV. Discover the zest of living. Involve your spouse (and children) in fun and games. Play charades, scrabble, board games, sports, anything that will bring you together. A happy family thrives on games, fun, and laughter.

3. TELL A JOKE

Laughter diffuses stress and tension. When you're in the midst of a bristling moment with your partner, look for a way out with the tool of humour. Ask yourself: What would a comedian do now? What would a clown do now? Then, play the part!

Try this daily affirmation: "I recognize that laughter is the best medicine for the daily aches and pains of married life."

ASK DADA

Is there ever a time when laughter is not appropriate? I like to joke around, but sometimes I'm not sure if making a joke during an argument will further upset my partner.

Make your wife or husband laugh in the middle of a fight and you'll show her your best side. But, make sure that the joke is at your expense! We must laugh with others, never at others. If we have to laugh at somebody, we must laugh at ourselves.

MEDITATION MOMENTS

It is impossible for you to be angry and laugh at the same time. Anger and laughter are mutually exclusive and you have the power to choose either.

~ Wayne Dyer

POWER UP YOUR DAY WITH YOUR OWN DAILY AFFIRMATION.

Today, I will choose to laugh when _____

_____.

The Ninth Secret...

Do Not Bottle Up Your Anger

If ever there is a misunderstanding, do not hide your feelings.

There are safe and appropriate ways to express anger in a loving relationship. Not by yelling or shouting. Not by pointing a finger. But by talking.

Therefore, discuss whatever is in your heart freely and without fear.

Communicate!

ASK DADA

Every time I try to talk to my husband about something, I start out calm but quickly spiral into a fighting voice. I've been meditating on what I can do to approach a conversation from a different place. Do you have any suggestions?

You must know yourself well before you communicate effectively with your partner. It has been said, "Two people begin to fight when they do not understand each other's language." What is referred to here is not the language of voice and words, but the language of the heart. Love. Know yourself. Assess your own strengths and weaknesses before you judge another person!

Is there such a thing as a loving argument?

Yes. When you express yourself in a firm yet positive manner, you are controlling the most negative aspects of anger. When approaching your partner to discuss something that made you angry or hurt, avoid negative suggestions and hostile judgments like, "You are selfish," or "You don't care." Stop judging and accusing one another. Simply talk about how something made you feel.

MEDITATION MOMENTS

Holding on to anger is like grasping a hot coal with the intent of throwing it at someone else; you are the one who gets burned.

~ **Buddha**

POWER UP YOUR DAY WITH YOUR OWN DAILY AFFIRMATION.

I allow myself to acknowledge angry feelings by

_____

_____

_____

The Tenth Secret...

PRAY TOGETHER

When the presence of God is asserted in a marriage, then the marriage is truly made in heaven. It becomes the supreme highway on which two linked souls walk toward one ultimate goal. They are linked to each other through golden chains of love, understanding, devotion, and piety.

If you want to build a happy home and family, bring God into your home. Every day, you must find some time to sit together and praise the Lord. Thank Him for having brought the two of you together.

THE TAKEAWAY

Happy marriages are not handed over to anyone on a silver platter. You have to work hard at them. But God can give you all the help and inspiration that you need!

God is the source of all that is good in life. He is the source of understanding, tolerance, insight, patience, and love. It is easy to acquire these virtues when you put yourself in His hands.

When you pray together, you draw in and restore peace, balance, and harmony to your marriage and family.

LIFE IMITATES ART

A man dreamt that he went up to the divine storehouse where God kept all the marvelous gifts that He bestows on mankind.

The man said to the angel in charge, "I'm sick and tired of the miseries, ill-will, and strife on earth. Can you give me love, joy, peace, and justice?"

The angel smiled. "We don't stock fruits here," he answered. "Only seeds."

Many of us today have thrown God out of our homes. This has created a vacuum—and when there is a vacuum created in life, the devil rushes in to fill it! Here are some suggestions for bringing God into your home.

1. PUT UP A BIG, BEAUTIFUL PORTRAIT OF YOUR *ISHT DEVA* OR A PICTURE OF GREAT SOUL WHO INSPIRES YOU

It could be Krishna, Rama, Buddha, Jesus, Guru Nanak, Baha'ullah, or any saint or savior of humanity who draws you. Put it in a prominent position in your house, preferably so that you can see it from the entrance. Every time any of you leave the home, bow in reverence, close your eyes, and offer a simple prayer.

2. IF YOU HAVE A PROBLEM OR DISAGREEMENT, TAKE IT TO GOD

If ever you have a disagreement or a problem, take it to God. Somehow a solution will come. When you take a disagreement or misunderstanding to God, you remove it from the realm of human bitterness. In God's presence we cannot argue with bitterness. In God's presence we cannot shout at each other. Surrender yourselves to God. Put your problems and difficulties before him. Seek guidance from Him. Not only in adversity, but at all times.

3. PRAY AS A FAMILY EVERYDAY

One way to do this is for a family to spend some time together daily in God's presence. Gather together all the members of the family from the oldest to the youngest for at least 15 minutes in God's presence and hold a brief 'prayer meeting'. You can sing the Lord's name, chant your favorite *mantra*, do a little *kirtan*, or have a reading from the scriptures or the words of your Guru. You can pick up a thought-for-the-day from a great thinker and each of you can say what you feel about it. If you can't do this together everyday, at least do this once a week.

4. SEE THE DIVINE IN YOUR PARTNER

In the Hindu tradition, the husband worships Devi (goddess) Herself in his wife. So, too, the wife worships God in her husband. When you imbibe this idea, you become conscious that God is within each one of us, and you love and serve God in the members of your family. This is a way of elevating human relationships, and making marriage and family life a means of moving toward God.

Try this daily affirmation: "We are poised and secure in God's presence, and our hearts are serene."

ASK DADA

When I got married, my friends warned me not to be too devoted to my spiritual goals and religious practices. They said that if I bring too much religion into our marriage, my husband will feel that I am neglecting him. Is this true?

It was Mother Teresa who said, "The family is the place to learn God. God created the family—together as husband, wife, and children—to reflect his Love." Being attuned to God or being devoted to spiritual goals does not mean that you will neglect your spouse and his needs or concerns! You can fulfill your duties and responsibilities in the marriage and be the ideal companion to your partner even while following the spiritual path. How? By beholding God in your spouse and offering love and respect and affection to him. Appreciate all that he is and all that he does. In marriage, you must seek to be the ideal, dedicated partner, a companion to your spouse in spiritual evolution. When a married couple lose sight of this high ideal, their marriage can be nothing more than a convenient arrangement. Any marriage that does not rise above motivations of physical desire, social advancement and financial considerations will become merely a bondage. When the spiritual element enters marriage, that marriage is truly made in heaven!

MEDITATION MOMENTS

One might estimate the weight of the world, tell the size of the celestial city, count the stars of heaven, measure the speed of lightning, and predict the time of the rising and setting sun. But you cannot even estimate the power of prayer. Prayer is as vast as God because He is behind it. Prayer is as mighty as God because He has committed Himself to answer it.

~ Leonard Raverhill

POWER UP YOUR DAY WITH YOUR OWN DAILY AFFIRMATION.

Lord, I pray for those closest to me — my family, my friends, my neighbours, my colleagues. What a blessing they are! Yet, all relationships bring challenges too. So, I ask specifically that_____

_____

_____

_____.